ENABLER'S JOURNEY RECOVERY PLAN

Enabler's Journey Recovery Series Book One

Angie G Meadow MSN; Perry Meadows MD, &
Sarah J Meadows BS

Abstract: This is book one of a recovery workbook series. It guides individuals or clients to understand enabling behaviors and evaluate their current participation in perpetuating the dysfunctional behaviors of a person with Substance Use Disorder. The enabler will learn to recognize the cycle of enabling, entanglement, excuses and beliefs that handicap an enabler from recovery. It also coaches in the courage needed to detach from uncontrollable destructive behaviors and circumstances. The book includes a recovery plan, accountability questionnaire, self-care program and a plan for identifying unhealthy and healthy coping strategies. It will also guide the recovering enabler to determine a level of safe involvement with a person with Substance Use Disorder and how to identify true and false recovery, rebuild trust, and avoid the snare of another enabling relationship.

A Thousand Tears, LLC

PO Box 561

Lewisburg, PA 17837

enablersjourney@gmail.com

www.enablersjourney.com

© 2019 Angie G. Meadows, Perry Meadows, and Sarah J. Meadows

This book is intended as general information only and should not be used to diagnose or treat any health condition. In light of the complex, individual, and specific nature of health problems, this book is not intended to replace professional medical advice. The ideas, procedures, and suggestions in this book are intended to supplement, not replace, the advice of a trained medical professional. Consult your physician before adopting any of the suggestions in this book, as well as about any condition that may require diagnosis or medical attention. The author and publisher disclaim any liability arising directly or indirectly from the use of this book.

This publication is designed to provide accurate and authoritative information with regard to the subject matter covered. It is sold with the understanding that the publisher is not engaged in rendering legal, accounting, or other professional advice. If legal advice or other expert assistance is required, the services of a competent professional person should be sought.

From a *Declaration of Principles* jointly adopted by a Committee of the American Bar Association and a Committee of Publishers and Associations.

Contents

PREFACE

This book gives no advice. It only gives information for observation, self-reflection and allows the enabler to set aside the confusion and make rational decisions based upon what is best for yourself and not what is best for people with unreasonable behaviors. The content is a compilation of our healing journey from a lifetime of observing addictive/abusive behaviors.

The main writer is Angie. My constant coaches and editors are Perry and Sarah. When going through this journey and hanging onto an imaginative dream of future success for our loved one, we were going financially deeper and deeper in debt. We realized the definition of insanity according to Alcoholic Anonymous is to continue to do the same thing again and again and expect different results. We had no choice but to stop or drown financially. We had to seek our own recovery from people and circumstances we could not control or change. While watching our loved ones suffer in addiction and enabling, we had no power to make a difference. At times, it was unbearable sorrow.

This book will help you develop courage, identify the safe levels of involvement with a person with irresponsible behaviors, work a recovery plan and avoid the pitfalls that are inevitable when seeking to untangle from unhealthy relationships and pursue a journey of health and well-being for yourself. This is not selfish. It is the kindest thing you could do for yourself or others. ***Healthy relationships make stable families.***

Consider all this information and use your best judgment to determine what works for you. Only you can identify what does or does not apply to your circumstances.

I use he/him to refer to the person with addictive/abusive behaviors. You may use whatever gender pronoun applies to your situation.

I use the word "person with substance use disorder" (SUD) to refer to our loved ones caught in any addictive behaviors. This could include the strongest street drugs, prescription medications, excessive use of alcohol, gambling, pornography, gaming, food addictions and a myriad of other things that may control our loved ones. This book shares how I have recovered from my impulsive enabling behaviors.

Although this book is written based upon our experience with individuals with Substance Use Disorder, the principles also apply to those caught in domestic violence and with other dysfunctional behaviors.

This is the second edition and has minor changes.

INTRODUCTION

"He's not sick, you are," said the woman at Al-Anon. Proceeding to defend my mental soundness with a horde of reasons, I described how I was the responsible one and not the "sick one". Smugly she responded, "Well, who keeps allowing the insanity to continue by interrupting the consequences."

Stunned at the realization that I was the "sick one", I implored her to speak to me about how any loving mother could reject involvement in their **adult child's** life. Particularly a momma who could foresee all the future ramifications of taking such a stance against his dysfunctional behaviors: financial devastation, unemployment, destruction of his health, loss of his home, divorce, abandoned and aborted children, imprisonment, and certain death and destruction are on this path.

She assured me all these consequences were looming possibilities. The consequences were more imminent with my excusing his irresponsible behaviors. Setting firm boundaries and not allowing myself to succumb to the emotional manipulation, was the only sane thing to do.

In my last weeping plea to her, I said, "Mothers don't turn their backs on their children." Quickly she retorted, "Yes, but those mothers don't have to deal with this garbage! We have to get tough and stop being part of the problem."

The realization that I was obsessed with saving my adult child with SUD set me on the path of recovery.

It has been a 28-year journey of analyzing my behaviors and the behaviors of others around me and documenting my observations. One of the greatest virtues I have learned is courage.

COURAGE to set firm boundaries against self-destructive absurdity and make my own decisions for a healthy future for me and the innocent ones under my care.

My decisions are not based on emotional manipulation from an out of control individual!

Eventually, I was able to let go of insanity and recover my own heart. Giving myself permission to move forward, I can now enjoy my own life. I can care for others in the wake of my loved one's destructiveness and bring healing to those who want help. I can release my loved one to the consequences of his own choices and hope that he will soon want to stop his suffering and also find recovery. Let's begin...

CHAPTER ONE

THE STAGES OF ENABLING

The Road to Acceptance Leads to Peace

An enabler is one who empowers another to persist in self-destructive behaviors, such as substance use, by providing excuses or by making it possible to avoid the consequences of such behavior. (Merriam-Webster, Inc. 2018) An enabler must realize they are not dealing with their rational loved one, but with one driven by the insatiable demon of addiction.

> *The only way to recover your loved one from this bondage is to recover yourself first.*

Elizabeth Kubler-Ross, in her work "On Death and Dying" identified the five stages of grief: 1. Denial 2. Anger 3. Bargaining 4. Depression and 5. Acceptance. As with grief upon the death of a loved one, enablers must go through the same stages to obtain freedom from the mental torment associated with enabling another adult with irresponsible addictive behaviors.

◆ ◆ ◆

Angie G Meadow MSN; Perry Meadows MD, & Sarah J Meadows BS

Denial

Whenever an enabler makes excuses, covers up, or accepts the financial consequences of another person's behaviors, it literally places them in denial. Soon, another crisis surfaces. The enabler must then decide whether to accept the situation or attempt to "fix it" and return to their denial. During this stage, one frequently reacts with shock, which results from an awareness of possible impending death due to the serious destructive behaviors of a loved one. Unfortunately, it is not a shock that might bring about change, but one where the enabler asks, "What will the other people think?" Or "I need to fix the problem and he will appreciate it so much, he won't do it again." **The enabler will often assist the person with SUD in the diversion of blame and escaping consequences.**

Do you rescue others from the consequences of their poor choices?

Does it help them? Or do they continue to make poor choices?

♦ ♦ ♦

Anger

Once an enabler has made a financial investment in helping their loved one, they become angry when the person with SUD is ungrateful and not making steps to change. The anger is particularly intense if the person with SUD starts stealing from them and continues lying to them. If there is no anger, the enabler is truly deceived, thinking their continual righteous acts of goodness will cover the unrighteous ones made by the one they are protecting. The enabler can be a soft target if they have unresolved guilt from the past.

Is there something that you regret from the past that causes you guilt and makes you feel obligated to rescue an individual from their consequences?

How often are you angry with your loved one? Has anger solved any of the issues long term?

♦ ♦ ♦

Bargaining

During this stage, the enabler becomes a manipulator for "good outcomes". But, a manipulator just the same and will begin preying on the good will of others, including friends and family, to "help" the individual with SUD. The manipulation by the enabler may involve lying or even threats in order to obtain assistance for their loved one. Then, the coercion extends to their loved one with SUD. This is a masterful skill to extort good behavior from their loved one with dysfunctional behaviors. Manipulation is then learned and perfected by their loved one; it is flipped back onto the enabler and used to fuel our exaggerated guilt to continue financial extortion.

Do you manipulate another to do what is right?

Do you manipulate others to rescue your loved one with SUD?

◆ ◆ ◆

Depression

When reality sets in and the enabler realizes they are not the one who can save their loved one with SUD and cannot manage another person's morality or actions, despair sets in. The enabler sinks into confusion and despair. They think they are being too harsh and rush to save their protégé to alleviate the depression. This continues the toxic relationship. In this stage, they have fallen into a repeating cycle of bewilderment, feeling helpless and hopeless. The tendency is to throw money at it and revert to the **stage of denial** and sweep the problems under the rug. **It is impossible to cure addiction issues with money.** Instead, you have received their financial consequences and they are free from responsibility. Now, their only care is the next high.

How often do you feel helpless and hopeless over a situation?

Do you go back to the stage of rescuing and enabling to stop anxiety or depression? This only moves you back to denial to restart the cycle.

◆ ◆ ◆

Acceptance

It is not until the enabler comes to an end of their coercing and realizes things are broken and beyond "their" control that they can find acceptance.

> *The enabler is powerless to change another and must let go of the responsibility to do so.*

How much courage and strength would it take to detach from another adult person's problems?

Detaching is followed by an extensively painful mourning period, which feels like a very long funeral dirge. In this process, the enabler must die to their own wishes and future goals for their loved one with SUD. This "emotional death" gives the enabler the freedom to live their life and invest themselves in others who can be safely loved and who want to enjoy healthy relationships.

This is a grieving process not understood by others. There is a constant impending doom or dread. It takes courage to grieve and detach from the responsibility for the outcomes of another adult person's choices.

This grieving makes us painfully aware of our helplessness. If we can grieve and detach from our desire to control outcomes, our relationship with a person with SUD will change. We will be able to recover ourselves and find our balance in life. We will be stronger and healthier. This, in turn, will end the relationship or mature the relationship to a healthier level.

> *When an enabler matures and develops healthy boundaries, the loved one with SUD may also desire recovery.*

The enabler must emotionally release the one they cannot save from his/her own compulsions. This is done by allowing them to experience the pain of consequences to their irresponsible decisions.

As a recovering enabler, do the research for them and give them addresses and phone numbers for substance disorder treatment centers, medication-assisted treatment clinics, sober living houses, food pantries, homeless shelters, and support groups. However, **the enabler must leave the decision of recovery in their loved one's hands.** Even a functional person with SUD with a home, car, and employment must be fully responsible for their financial obligations. Allowing them to wallow in the pigpen of consequences might wake them up to the reality of the future they are destroying and become a catalyst for change.

So, my fellow enablers, could this mean death of our loved one? Absolutely! Addictions can certainly lead to death.

> *Enablers do not need to stay on the path of destruction with their loved one.*
>
> *The enabler must realize their over-responsibility is fostering their loved one's under-responsibility.*

Let your loved one learn responsibility for their actions quickly while they are young. Let them bear the brunt of full responsibility for their legal and financial issues. When they experience very painful circumstances, they may choose to change. **If you rescue, the next consequence of your loved one's actions will be more destructive and maybe even life threatening.**

The road of an enabler is mental torment and despair.

The road of acceptance leads to peace.

DYSFUNCTIONAL ENABLER CYCLE

This book will begin to assist us to explore the toxic behaviors of addiction and our corresponding dysfunctional behaviors. Until we can clearly see the game the addictive substances drive our loved ones to play, we cannot break the cycles of enabling.

This cycle can be broken at any time through acceptance. The way to stop an enabler's suffering of this repetitive cycle is to accept the choices our adult loved one with SUD is making for their own lives. Then, we can use our energy o choose the level of involvement we want in this relationship.

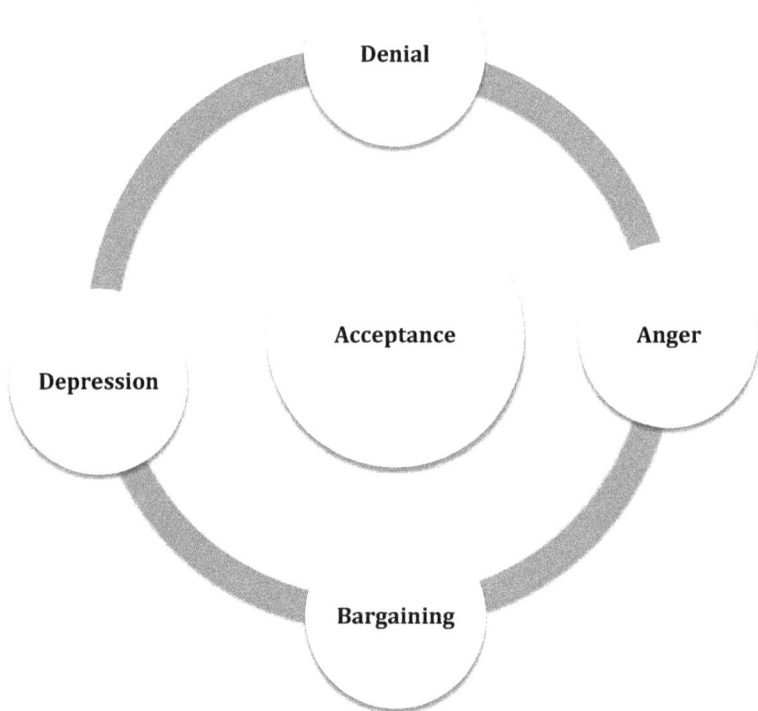

Denial

Acceptance

Anger

Depression

Bargaining

LEVELS OF INVOLVEMENT

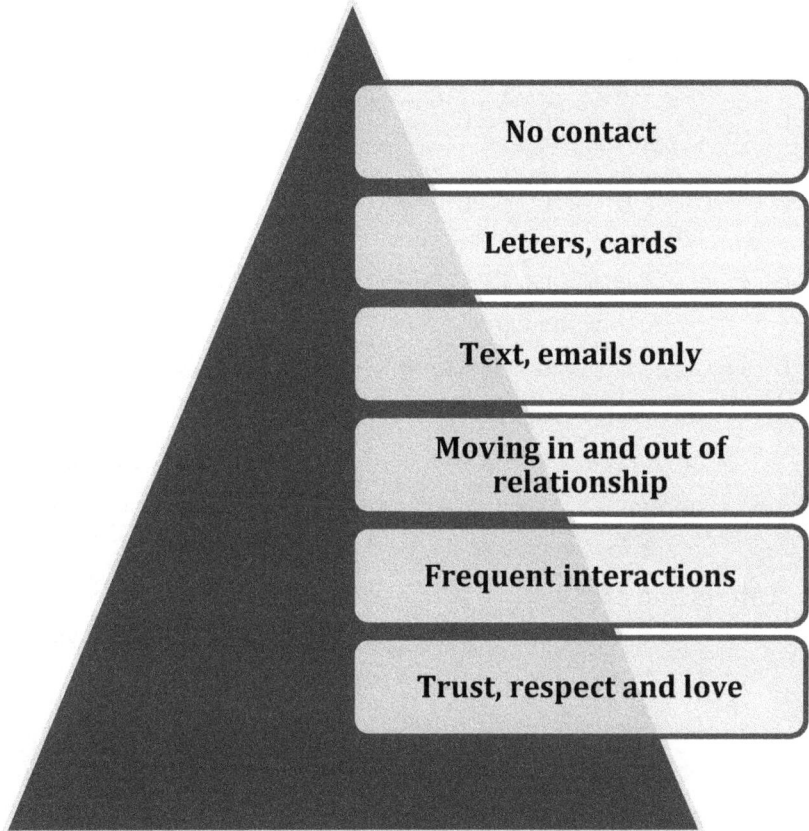

No contact

Letters, cards

Text, emails only

Moving in and out of relationship

Frequent interactions

Trust, respect and love

When we are entangled in a relationship with active enabling behaviors, think, space and distance. Move back in the relationship to a safe and comfortable level. If the relationship is still causing stress and anxiety, move back further. Your inner circle should be reserved for people who have earned the right to be there.

No contact

- When a person with substance use disorder is blaming everyone else for their problems and refusing personal responsibility, they need the space to sit with the consequences of their own decisions. This will look different in different situations. It also may be temporary. It could last for a few hours, days or even need to last a year or more. Always receive counseling or group support at this level.
- Always establish accountability and relationship rules before re-entering this relationship.
- If they are lying, stealing, manipulating, bullying or will not listen to reason, you need space to heal.
- A key to the necessity of this measure being exercised is when the relationship has turned to *total torment*. You can't think of anything else and it wakes you up at night with fear, anxiety or misery. For your own safety and sanity, create distance and space for yourself to heal.

Letters and cards

- This is a space where the relationship is valuable, and you would like to keep the door open for future healing.
- Or reconciliation isn't likely, but you would like to show continued love and support without enabling or being wounded physically or emotionally.

Text and emails only

- Some loved ones caught in addiction and enablers are so relationally dependent that there is constant, compulsive enabling in the relationship, for your sake, distance is needed.

Moving in and out of relationship

- This space is for a person who is learning to manage their emotions.

- Anyone who reacts, responds or makes decisions based upon emotions need a strong, dependable loved one to say, "You may not engage me until you have worked through these emotions, then we can talk."
- Sometimes exaggerated emotions are justified, and they need to talk through the confusion of the day, but if the emotions are being used to violate the trust in the relationship or build a case to manipulate you emotionally, there needs to be distance.

Frequent Interactions
- This is a space for loved ones with SUD who are finding their recovery path in life. They need encouragement and emotional support and direction, but also need the space to build self-confidence.
- This space will allow our loved ones to reach out to counselors, sponsors, and valuable mentors to develop other healthy relationships.

Trust, Respect, and Love
- Do not allow anyone into your inner circle who cannot be fully trusted.
- Do not allow anyone in your inner circle who does not respect your opinion, decisions and boundaries.
- Do not give your love away to someone who will trample it and abuse you.

GET THE FACTS QUESTIONNAIRE

Distance from the unteachable. Answer Yes or No.

1) Does this person attempt to control my thoughts? Usually he does this by repeating himself continually and getting louder and louder.	
2) Does this person dominate or regulate my actions? He tells me where I can go and who I can or cannot see.	
3) Is there a repeated pattern of abuse?	
4) Does this person attempt to make themselves financially dependent on me or entangle me financially with joint bank accounts, co-signing, etc.?	
5) Does this person have constant excuses for why they can't work or can't keep a job?	
6) Does their money disappear everyday: fee, fine, robbery, suspicious expenses?	
7) Does this person lie to me or steal from me?	
8) Are others, who love me, concerned about my over involvement with this person?	
9) Do they flatter and smile to get my devotion?	
10) Do they act helpless and come to me to rescue them?	
11) Do they dominate my time and isolate me from other relationships?	
12) Do they manipulate with unstable emotions (crying, pleading, anger, etc.)	

Most importantly: Am I free to say "NO" to them without repercussions?

IDENTIFYING ADDICTIVE AND ENABLING BEHAVIORS

Addictive Behaviors	Enabling Behaviors
Manipulation	Merciful/Tender-hearted
Lying	Fixer
Stealing	Over-responsible
Cheating	People pleaser
Blaming	Desires good outcomes
Coercing	Manipulates for good
Hiding/Cowardly	Assist the person with
Obsessive thinking	addictive behaviors:
Compulsive/Impulsive	Blaming
Negative thinking	Making Bail
Grumbling/Complaining	Motivated by guilt
Pretending helplessness	Gullible
Immature	Philosophy is to keep picking
Raging	them up until they can stand.
Bullying	Believes money can fix the
Anger	problem.
Abusive	Believes consequences are
Irresponsible	unfair or harsh.
Crisis making	Fearful
Diverting the attention	Anxious and Stressed
elsewhere	Denies the addiction is real
Separating enablers from	Feels no one loves their
others	loved one in addiction but them
Gossip/slanders anyone	Thinks they are the loved
who opposes them	one's savior

Isolating or Peer dependent	Thinks if they fix the temporary consequence one more time, their loved one will stop their addictive patterns Denial/Excuse maker

CHAPTER TWO

COURAGE TO STOP THE ENABLING

Courage is not an accidental character trait.

Courage is mental or moral strength to venture, persevere, and withstand danger, fear, or difficulty (Merriam-Webster, Inc. 2018) We develop courage by choosing courageous responses over fearful ones. Enablers need courage to withstand fear and difficulties. If we allow natural consequences to one's poor choices quick and early, our loved ones may not get so deeply entangled in addiction. Instead, let us recognize difficulties as a blessing to teach us and our loved ones to quickly avoid the destructive path of addiction.

COURAGE IS MENTAL AND MORAL STRENGTH	
Persevering to find recovery: substance use, enabling, or any other addictive pattern	
Diligent to develop a plan and stick to it	
Refusing stress, worry and anxiety continually throughout the day.	

Fearless of the future and hopeful	
Refusing the luxury of self-pity	
Brave enough to do the right thing	
Tenacious enough to say "no" to yourself	
Exercising strong boundaries with others	
NO FEAR for anyone else's consequences of their poor choices	
Determined to focus on your own self and change your own dysfunctional behavior patterns.	
Courageous enough to look at your past wounds	
Not able to be emotionally manipulated	
Making all decisions with your mind and not emotions	
Not able to be offended; or recognizes offenses and moves through them quickly. If this isn't done, you will be stuck in a negative thinking pattern.	
Never cheats, lies or steals	
Doesn't make excuses for others	
Doesn't make excuses for self	
Open and accountable	
Not afraid to reach out for support, or emotional counseling. Admits powerlessness over another.	
Not afraid to get legal counsel and follow through	
Not afraid to detach from someone who refuses to be accountable for their poor decisions.	
Pursuing Virtue: Love, hope and peace	

When you DISENGAGE from the chaos of toxic relationships, you may be considered the enemy.

DEALING WITH OTHER ENABLERS WHEN YOU STOP ENABLING

- The whole family may dive in and enable the person with SUD. Expect to be accused of being uncaring and cold hearted. You are only valuable if you can be used or manipulated.
- The person with SUD may slander and destroy your character, exaggerate your past failures, and flip the meaning of your words.
- It becomes gut-wrenching to watch the lunacy, the lies, the manipulation, the confusion of impending squandering of life savings of elderly enablers, or your future inheritance.
- It is like watching a train wreck that cannot be stopped.
- At this point, **your anxiety will match the level of involvement you continue to have with the person with SUD and the other toxic enablers.**
- Even if you have no verbal contact, your anxiety may still be very high. In order to decrease and stop the anxiety, you must emotionally detach.
- If there are elderly or unsuspecting honest people being consistently conned, we might keep some contact with them to speak truth and be the voice of reason.
- You must stay emotionally detached and **never give them cash**: the person with SUD or enablers.
- If you enable an enabler and pay their bills, you have just enabled them to continue enabling the loved one with SUD without any consequences of their own.
- It may take a decade for the prime enabler to be completely bankrupt and lose everything, but this is the path they are choosing.
- Do not pay off the loans for prime enablers or they will have good credit

and obtain more loans.

- If an elderly enabler is now frail or having signs of dementia, and you choose to take them into your home, a **"No contact"** rule must be in place between them and anyone in active addiction.
- Formerly honest enablers may lose their senses and rob other family members and friends. They may, also, turn a blind eye when the their loved one with SUD steals.
- Do not loan an enabler money for their bills if they have not repaid what they previously borrowed from you.
- You must understand most enablers are as addicted to enabling as the person with SUD is to their substance of choice. It is the enabler's way of attempting to "control" outcomes.
- The rescuing has become their identity and enablers live in pseudo-reality. Enabler's have a fairytale thinking. They think their enabling will result in a life free from pain.
- The enabler's toxic relationship with their loved one with SUD is an unhealthy love.
- Even if they see the lies and manipulation, they may choose to cover it up or continue excusing it.
- Reconciliation is extended to the person with SUD without requiring any restitution, accountability, or lasting behavioral changes.
- They are sacrificing themselves for their loved one with SUD and feel it is a noble cause.
- The enabler cannot coddle or bribe the person with SUD into changing.
- Unfortunately, the enabler and their loved one with SUD both need tough consequences.
- It is difficult to legally prove an enabler with early signs of dementia is being abused. If they have freely given money away to this loved one with SUD in the previous decade, it is especially difficult to prove they are not acting out of "free will". They may be having

hundreds of dollars a day embezzled. The person with SUD soon preys on the memory loss and uses the same excuse for the need of money in the evening as they used in the morning.

- It may be appropriate with the elderly in early dementia to attempt to contact elder abuse or an attorney to get control over the estate and finances.
- This is a devastating and depressing end for 70-80-year old.
- We need to have the legal power to contact the credit bureau or the elderly will be conned into taking out loans and eventually be unable to meet their payments and lose everything.
- If the money is gone by the 2nd or 3rd of every month, instruct the enabler where the food pantries are located.
- If they give their car to their loved one with SUD, let them ride a bus or save money for a taxi. Only give them a ride if it is convenient and is something you would have normally done.
- The sooner an enabler loses everything, and their credit is ruined, the sooner they will be forced to stop. Beware, the primary enabler will also become more desperate and try a myriad of tactics to extort money from you to save their loved one with SUD.
- Don't get things out of the pawn shop or you will need to do it every month. If you do retrieve an item out of the pawn shop, keep control over it.
- Sometimes, all you can do is prepare your heart for a destitute parent, grandparent, or sibling.
- If there is domestic violence, child abuse, neglect, or endangerment, seek further counsel.

FOR YOURSELF

- Get yourself healthy. Go to support groups and counseling.
- Learn good boundaries and how to say "NO" firmly.
- If the elderly or other enablers become destitute, you can decide how or how not to intervene. Sometimes you have to let them go on Medicaid and to a nursing home or they will bring the chaos in your home and will continue their enabling by giving all their pension or Social Security check away and expecting you to care for them financially and physically. I give you permission to say "no" and place conditions on your finances and on your physical availability to care for them.
- If you take an enabler in your home, they must be accountable to you for their money or find another place to live.
- Sometimes, the elderly enabler with mild-moderate dementia needs to be hidden from the others with dysfunctional addictive behaviors.
- If there are no enablers, you may have an opportunity to intervene with the person with SUD to arrange for confinement in a facility.
- If this doesn't work, you may need to leave your loved one with SUD in the streets and attempt to intervene to provide rehabilitation opportunity about once a month, until he is done with the streets and ready to do the work of recovery. This is very dangerous and needs to be a last resort with hard-core addiction behaviors. (A safer option would be to work with the authorities to incarcerate your loved one until he is sober and ready to work a recovery plan.)
- The cost of stopping your participation in this lunacy may be relationships with your mother, father, step-parent(s), siblings, children, spouse, etc. Stand firm! If you can get one or two loved ones to stop enabling, the others may learn quicker.
- At the very least, you can reclaim your life. Turn your focus onto children, friends or other loved ones who have been neglected.

CHAPTER THREE

THE ENABLER PARADIGM

The whole addiction process falls apart without a primary enabler.

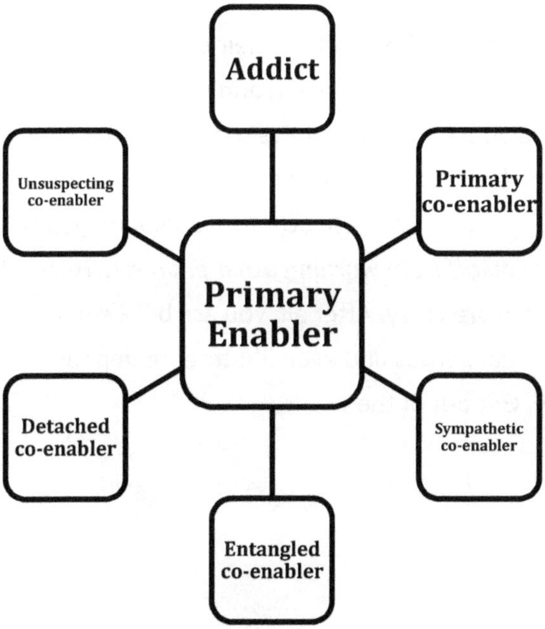
Addict
Unsuspecting co-enabler
Primary co-enabler
Primary Enabler
Detached co-enabler
Sympathetic co-enabler
Entangled co-enabler

Now, I want you to profile the players. If you can see what you are dealing with logically, you will be less likely hooked into the emotions of the game.

PROFILING

The Person with SUD: The Con

Con-man game

- o Nice
- o Sweet
- o Pleasant
- o Helpless, etc.

If you say no, or call them out on their emotionally manipulative kindness, the con man plays the victim and you are the abuser. Soon, they create havoc and you are cut out of the triangle with emotional/relationship suicide. *Emotional/relationship suicide is where you are railed, bullied and then ostracized by the person with SUD to manipulate you with intense emotions or cut you off from warning other enablers.* They will convince the other enablers you are crazy. After all, you are between them and their next high. This can be dangerous and even life threatening for you and can escalate quickly. Get out of the way!

The Characteristics of SUD

- Bully
- Belligerent

- Argumentative
- Thief
- Slanderer, etc.

Most likely this person cannot receive help until they are confined in prison (without an enabler bailing them out, making excuses, and hiring an attorney). This event could turn out to be the stimulus they need to propel them into recovery program with court accountability.

Protect your identity or it could be stolen as payback.

PRIME ENABLER

- Obsessed with their loved one with SUD and how to rescue them from consequences of poor choices
- Passive/aggressive
- Manipulative with loved one with SUD as well as their co-enablers
- Can praise or rail their co-enablers based upon their enabling assistance
- Bribing for good behavior
- Blaming everyone for their loved one's problems
- Lying and yet believes every lie their loved one tells them, even if they know it to be a lie
- Sneaky and secretive financially
- Unstable boundaries
- Trust in money to fix problems
- May truly desire to stop enabling, but they are relationally controlled by their loved one with SUD.

Prime enablers will keep others on the hook to help enable. The primary enabler uses and abuses others to benefit their loved one with SUD. They claim they are being abused by you when your enabling stops. When the enabler is bankrupt, they may blame a spouse or prey on other innocent family members until others are also bankrupt. *Blaming others is becoming a honed skill. Prime enablers are masters at playing the victim.* They focus on the current temporal problem. This enabler cuts off anyone they can't use to help enable their loved one with SUD to remain comfortable.

The primary enabler's life is characterized by cyclical confusion and denial of the root issues. **Love them from a distance with your head and not your heart or you may get sucked into the game again and again.**

There can be two primary enablers. A mother and grandmother of an adult child can both share in the responsibility of primary enabler. The two primary enablers will let the person with SUD bounce back and forth between them. The two primary enablers will convince each other of their loved one's good intentions, not understanding their loved one's inability to follow through without working a recovery plan. They will keep each other blind to the reality of their adult child's addiction.

Enablers may even have lucid moments when they understand what they are doing is wrong and swear they will never do it again. In order to recover, primary enablers must take steps to work a recovery plan and to be accountable financially to people who can be trusted to make right decisions for them.

> *The primary enabler is obsessed with their loved one with SUD.*

CO-ENABLERS

Primary Co-Enabler

(Spouse, parent, step-parent, grandparent, adult child, sibling, domestic partner, etc.)

This unhealthy relationship allows the prime enabler to play the victim with others in the family by claiming some of the other co-enablers are greedy, controlling and don't love the family member with SUD and won't care for their needs. (Albeit, the financial support is going for drugs and the primary co-enabler is usually aware of this scenario.)

The primary enabler and primary co-enabler can have great conflict. This sets the stage for sympathetic enablers to feel sympathy towards the primary enabler.

The co-enabler may also have addiction issues. They can be functional, able to work and manage finances. Often, they will escalate conflict, so they have an excuse to use their substance of choice. Usually this is a socially acceptable substance like prescription pills or alcohol.

> *The co-enabler doesn't see their own issues, but focus on the one with SUD as being the main problem.*

Passive/Aggressive Primary Co-enablers:

- Can be very responsible at times and then very irresponsible.
- Can perpetuate multiple conflicts with the one with SUD and primary enabler. This may give them an excuse to drink or use excessive prescription medications if they have addictive issues.
- Co-enablers may have substance use problems, if so, the guilt usually drives them to appease the primary enabler by giving financially to enable the loved one with addiction issues.
- Often, they love the primary enabler very much and assist in enabling to keep the peace and show support.
- When they realize the gravity of the impending financial doom,

they can rant obsessively.

- The primary and co-enabler's relationship is so out of balance that it could escalate to domestic violence or even homicide.
- Can also pretend to wholeheartedly enable the loved one with SUD, but the motive could be out of malice to attempt to finance an "accidental" overdose.
- Can also be unaware of root addiction issues and sincerely be trying to remedy the one with SUD's chronic bad luck.

Primary co-enablers are relationally dependent and not strong enough to walk away.

Sympathetic Co-Enabler

- Believe everything the primary enabler says.
- Defends the primary enabler.
- Takes pity on the primary enabler, because the primary enabler plays like they are abused and used. Primary Enablers usually have distressful financial consequences. The primary enabler is compelled to rescue and assume responsibility for their loved one with SUD and the sympathetic co-enabler frequently doesn't seem to understand the depth of this behavior.
- Tries to keep up with the primary enabler's doctor and dental bills.
- May even make sure their wants are supplied: eating out, hair dye, and other comfort items.
- May buy flowers and little gifts to comfort the primary enabler and cheer them up.

The primary enabler is believable because he/she is telling what they think is truth, but their reality is skewed by lies and manipulation. Primary enablers are deceived and deceive the sympathetic co-enabler.

The primary enabler sets up an offense between other co-enablers and anyone who won't play the game. This diverts the attention from the main issue (the irresponsible behaviors of the one with SUD) and this causes chaos and confusion.

The primary enabler emotionally manipulates co-enablers for money. They justify this by thinking their loved one will soon recover from addiction and it will be worth any sacrifice. The hard-luck stories are worthy of a Hollywood movie.

The sympathetic co-enablers listen and sympathize to the primary enabler's skewed reality.

> The primary enabler is never confronted and challenged to admit their dysfunctional behaviors.

All the focus is on the problems of the one with SUD or on the conflict with other co-enablers. If you discuss the primary enabler's dysfunctional behaviors and equitable consequences, they are quick to defend and blame.

Entangled Enabler

- Is one who has completely ceased to participate in enabling activities but is still relationally connected with the prime enabler.
- Needs to be aware that the primary enabler and one with SUD may plot to ruin them financially and destroy their reputation.
- If you choose to stay, prepare yourself.
- They may:
  - Call the police and falsify or exaggerate domestic violence

reports
- o Hurt themselves and say you did it
- o Rob your financial accounts
- o Steal your car
- o Pawn your multi-generational coin collection and tools and then blame you
- o Give away all your belonging to flea market dealer for a couple hundred dollars
- o Sell your $2,000 electronics for $100 while you are out of town
- o Act sweet one moment and be a snake to you the next
- o Accuse you of abusing them when you confront them about their dysfunctional behaviors
- o Blame you for the person with SUD's problems
- o Poison your food/drink
- o Find ways to blackmail you

If an entangled enabler stays to protect the primary enabler from the person with SUD, he/she is relationally dependent in a dysfunctional way.

The entangled enabler may have a fear of being alone, need to be needed or be deluded into thinking he can control the situation if he stays. The primary enabler will be aggressive and bullying, if the entangled enabler doesn't respond with sympathy to the loved one caught in addiction. Consider the possibility that the entangled enabler needs protection from the primary enabler and the person with SUD.

Sometimes an entangled enabler will stay with a primary enabler to attempt to protect them from the person with SUD. If you are an entangled enabler and choose to stay, disconnect emotionally and make decisions based upon what is best for you. Go to support group meetings and counseling to help unravel the confusion and to receive support for your decisions.

Detached Enabler

- Continues emotionally supporting other co-enablers.
- Is emotionally detached from the loved one with SUD and the primary enabler and recovering.
- Has begun practicing healthy boundaries and developing healthy relationships.
- Usually has been a primary enabler and has done several years of recovery work.
- Sees the issues and the dysfunction clearly.
- Motive for staying connected to co-enablers is to assist them in recovery.

Caution:

If you stay involved with other co-enablers who refuse to disentangle from toxic relationships physically, financially and/or emotionally, you will continue to experience emotional trauma which may harm your recovery. Also, if other co-enablers disrespect your boundaries, this will interrupt your recovery.

The more involved the detached enabler is:

- The more blame they will receive for the loved one with SUD's circumstances and consequences.
- The more likely they are to become entangled again.
- The less likely they will be able to develop healthy relationships.

Unsuspecting Co-Enablers

This is to WARN unsuspecting co-enablers about the behaviors of a primary enabler.

- **Doctors** – to convince them of his need for pain meds.
- **Lawyers** – to convince them of the injustice done for minor work injuries, slip and falls, minor car wrecks, or poor outcomes of medical procedures. Primary enabler will hire lawyers to convince the court their loved one with SUD is innocent of criminal charges. Primary enabler assists in filing for worker's compensation benefits and later disability benefits.
- **Insurance companies** – to falsify testimony for the car wrecked the previous night.
- **Police** – to falsify reports on the co-enablers that are hindering the enabling.
- **Probation officers** – to convince them of his outstanding improvement and his lack of need for accountability.
- **Child support authorities** – to insist his whereabouts are unknown.
- **Court authorities** – primary enabler will intervene on warrants and claim to be a guardian and make payments and do without their own needs being met. They will post bail.
- **Magistrates and Judges** – to convince them that he fulfilled his nine-month rehabilitation program in four months. Primary enabler will show up in court as his representative. Meanwhile, their loved one is hung over and unable to get out of bed.
- **Employers** – to give false references for him. They will call him off work.
- **Banks** – to cover all bad check charges and false deposit ATM claims.
- **Credit card companies** – to insist their identity was stolen again and they don't know who charged $4,000 of drugs from overseas again.

- **Neighbors** – to coerce in giving them daily transportation.
- **Sunday school friends** – to go to their homes at midnight and borrow "emergency" money.
- **Benevolence fund from the church** – to say he is dying and needs money for treatment.
- All potential **new lovers** are reeled in quickly with affirmation and adoration from the primary enabler. It is hopeful that a new enabler will emerge, and the primary enabler can have a break.

Conclusion:

- **If the primary enabler is providing for a person with SUD, don't provide for them.**
- **If you live with a primary enabler and/or one in active addiction, it will be a war zone.**
- **There is no recovery if there is no accountability.**
- **These are painful relationships to be in or even to watch from a distance.**

CHAPTER FOUR

TEN TYPES OF ADDICTION

*Addictions are often birthed from festering
unresolved emotional wounds.*

Addictions not only cause suffering; addictions are often birthed from festering unresolved emotional wounds. *We can ask forgiveness for our part in causing wounds and be an example by working on our own recovery.*

These next ten levels of addiction are the ones I have personally observed. As you read them, evaluate which level of unhealthy behaviors you and your loved one's exhibit. Then, you will be able to understand the level of dysfunction wherein you are contending.

Hard-core Addiction

Driven by impulse and lack of self-control

This individual with SUD will lie, cheat, steal from every employer, friend or family member. They may rob and bankrupt their elderly grandparents or make fraudulent worker's compensation claims. Others cut, stab and burn themselves to manipulate ER doctors for pain medications. They may steal the identity of other friends and family for credit card fraud. Previously, they have robbed employers and lack dependability and are now unemployable. It is not unusual for them to have abandoned children and beaten mates in their past. Often, they have a long criminal history and started drugs at an early age. They are extremely stubborn and difficult to help. They have paranoia and can be unpredictable with others who stand between them and their addictive substance of choice. These individuals are master manipulators. They can be innocent and helpless with an individual one moment, then fraudulently embezzle money, or rage and bully with a gun or a knife the next. They are very dangerous.

This person's ancestors usually have a long history of addiction issues. They may also have a co-morbidity with other behavioral health issues. They may have been neglected or abandoned by their father (and/or mother), and raised by a single-parent, grandparent or someone else. They are greatly lacking in self-control and are driven by impulse and emotions. They may be grandiose with narcissistic traits. They may have many self-destructive behaviors such as cutting, illicit sex, or other high-risk behaviors. They are frequently IV users and there is no drug they won't chase. Usually, they only slow down when they feel the full effect of severe consequences. As soon as they become comfortable (fed, clothed, warm and dry), they can find no self-control to be sober. This person may want to stop but has no power to do so. This individual with hard-core addiction issues need to be incarcerated to protect others and to be protected from themselves. Then, they may be willing to work a recovery program in lieu of a prison term.

Functional Addiction

Driven by guilt and shame

This person is fainthearted and lacks maturity or needs emotional healing from past trauma. They can be veterans who cannot reconcile war as a righteous act. They drink to medicate their conscious. They may have had an abortion and are struggling to forgive themselves for this or something else in their past. They could be stuck in a mourning stage over the death of a loved one or a bad divorce. Vacillating between blaming themselves and blaming others is common. They can usually maintain employment, but, have very poor coping skills and struggle in relationships. Keeping up appearances becomes more important than admitting they need help.

Overwhelmed Fainthearted

Driven by fear of failure

They lack confidence, feel inferior and isolate themselves. They often are hard workers and others take advantage of them. Their addiction keeps them from healthy relationships. Frequently, they whine and feel helpless or are loud, obnoxious and verbally abusive. They can be very depressed. This gives them an excuse to shut down real life and go into addiction behaviors to cope. They cycle into abusing others and being abused by others.

History of severe childhood abuse

Driven by emotional immaturity

They are numbing the pain. Physically, sexually, emotionally abused, or neglected and abandoned children can grow up to have chronic physical and emotional pain. They are difficult to treat because the root issues need time to surface and are hidden by a myriad of social issues that takes precedence.

Codependent/Enabler

Driven by a desire to "save" or "fix" others.

This person finds his/her identity in helping others. They also have the philosophy that if you just keep picking up an individual, they will eventually stand. They are sacrificing themselves and their financial stability for the "love" of another. ***This is an immature sick love.*** They can be passive/aggressive when they feel like doormats. Eventually, this "over responsibility" for a person with SUD makes them destitute and a burden on others. Frequently, they lose the very relationship they sought to save or become trapped in abuse. They don't understand addiction issues and think they can fix what is broken in their loved one by rescuing them from consequences. They often "enable" to stop the emotional pain they feel for their loved one or their social embarrassment over the situation. They also think more money can "fix" any problem. *If this person gets free from an abusive relationship and doesn't diligently work a recovery program for themselves, they will unknowingly hook into another abusive relationship attempting to resolve their past in the present.* They end up with different people, different names and faces, but the exact same scenarios of abuse. *Codependent/enablers tend to give themselves to people who are emotionally unavailable.*

Leech/Sponge

Driven by lack of morals and laziness
This person seems to be the party animal. They look for

financially stable people to attach themselves to and then work their "magic charm" to become entangled financially or emotionally with him/her (by marriage, having a child together, or a business deal). Once they have them entangled, they dominate and control by emotions, manipulation, confusion, chaos, blaming and an assortment of lies and pseudo-reality.

Dry Drunk or Workaholic

Driven by exaggerated, immature, unstable emotions

These individuals find their identity in their reputation and in their work ethic. They may be recovering from addiction and have not dealt with their emotional issues. They could be reputable professionals who work 16-18 hours a day. They have difficulty saying no to themselves and are frequently frustrated. They can be tyrants and oppress others (especially children, mates or co-workers). **They are addicted to raging, bullying or complaining.** These behaviors give them an allure of power and seems to temporarily release the pent up unresolved emotional pain of the past. They have many behaviors of a person with substance use disorders: **blaming, coercing, manipulating, bargaining, and denial.** Since they aren't prone to numbing their emotions with mind altering substances, they have lots of energy to work themselves up into a fretful frenzy. These individuals can be prone to physically or emotionally beat and batter their enablers. They tend to be control freaks and feel very empty and lonely and have trust issues. Yet, they erroneously see themselves as very healthy individuals because of their accomplishments or their bank account. They might also struggle with varying degrees of behavioral health issues.

Helpless dependency addiction

Driven by inner fears and brokenness

This person may have a chronic illness, car accident or a work injury. They may hate pain medication, but, are caught in a pain cycle. They are unable to cope with the withdrawal to stop the prescription medications. They need emotional stability and other alternatives to relieve the pain. Usually, they have a great need to learn boundaries and to nurture and care for themselves.

Dual Addictions: Sub-Addictions can run simultaneously with dominate addictions.

Entertainment Addiction

Driven by peer pressure, self-consciousness

This person attaches to food, games, computers, phones, television shows or actors and binges when they feel lonely or overwhelmed. They also struggle feeling connected or give their loyalty to the wrong people. They may be fearful of connection and avoid eye contact during conversation by watching their phones while their mates, children, family or friends attempt to engage them. They are inordinately afraid to move forward, even in safe environments. Often procrastination and complacency, prevents this person from achieving the goals they desire to accomplish. This person has not accomplished a solid identity. They have difficulty saying no and lack the confidence to establish healthy boundaries. Their insecurities lead to physical illnesses and psychosomatic pain syndromes. Some of this seems the norm in the teens and early 20's, but this is not a stage you would want to be stuck in.

41

Love and Sex Addiction

Driven by lack of self-control or attachment disorders

This person connects through sexual intimacy. They have weak impulse control and/or are addicted to the hunt and the rush of a new partner. They do not know how to love or become truly intimate in a relationship to bring about the emotional fulfillment they truly desire. They were not affirmed as a child or may have been over indulged. They may have been orphans or in foster care. Even if their family unit was intact, their identity was most likely not established; therefore, they attach to sensual indulgences. They may have developed a habit of fantasy thinking or indulged pornography early in life to escape reality. Their need to satisfy their cravings is higher than their need to be responsible in their behaviors towards others. They have great difficulty being quiet or alone. They may have difficulty sleeping at night.

Conclusions:

Individuals with SUD cannot identify the root issue(s) and are moody, broody and depressive and are attempting to medicate themselves instead of learning healthy coping skills. **Self-pity and negative thinking mental loops** are common and racing thoughts can reign supreme. Yet some individuals with SUD have no cognitive awareness, but, attempt to micro-manage their lives by controlling other people or every temporal thing in their environment. Other individuals may be extremely careless and throw all caution to the wind and live recklessly.

Easily Identified

Hard Core Addiction: Impulse and lack of self-control

Functional Addiction: Guilt and Shame

Fainthearted: fear of failure

Emotional Immaturity: Childhood Trauma/abuse

Codependent/Enabler: Over responsible and fixer

Leech/Sponge: Lack of morals/laziness

Dry drunk/workaholic: exaggerated unstable

Helpless dependency: inner fears and brokenness

Entertainment: Peer pressure/self-consciousness

Love and Sex Addiction: Lack self-control or attachment disorders

Most individuals with SUD live a life characterized by the imbalance of undisciplined thinking and exaggerated immature emotions resulting in self-destructive behaviors.

These behavioral patterns keep them in an emotional whirlwind and dominates every area of their lives and leaves them feeling empty.

The younger a person engages in addiction behaviors as a coping skill, the more stunted their emotional development. A seventy-year old man can still be throwing fits like a four-year old. A thirty-year old who started drugs at the age of twelve may still developmentally be a young adolescent.

This is a sampling of the different reasons I have observed for addictions. I am certain there are many more. Many of these reasons overlap. The more reasons for addiction identified in our lives, the more unraveling that needs to be done.

> *Addictions make our relationships and home environments unstable. This instability diverts our attention from the root issues and fuels our perpetual suffering.*

Recovery will achieve great momentum when the answers become visibly achievable and we can separate healthy and unhealthy behaviors clearly. The bulk of this process takes 1-2 years. When we find community, hold each other accountable and teach it to others, our recovery becomes more stable. **But have no delusions, this is work.**

CHAPTER FIVE

SELF-EVALUATION

Until we can evaluate our losses and gains, we cannot understand where we have been and the work we need to do to arrive at where we want to go.

What were the circumstances from childhood or early adulthood that could be the root causes for addictive behaviors and/or dysfunctional coping skills? I would like for you to name all the destructive influences of your childhood. Add any other circumstances not listed that may have caused you instability or an emotional wound.	
Identify Childhood Set up:	Yes/ no
Domestic Violence	
Abandoned	

Neglected	
Brain Washed	
Incest/Rape	
Enabling parent	
Verbally abusive parent	
Alcoholic in the home	
Substance use disorder	
Severe street drug use	
Homelessness	
Divorce	
Unable to please parents	
Not validated	
Not safe	
Unable to feel comforted/loved	
Promiscuous parent	
Parental marital conflict	
Single Parent	
No parent	
Emotionally absent parent	

Incarcerated parent	
Abusive siblings	
Bullying peers	
Given drugs or alcohol at a young age	
Other:	
2) What are the outcomes you can identify from your emotional childhood pain? It is important to understand the consequences of this negativity. Add any insight to your list. **Outcome:**	
Confusion	
Fear	
Anxiety	
Stubbornness	
Rebellion	
Misplaced values	
Poor decision maker	
Habitual liar	
Negative thinking or racing thoughts	

Exaggerated emotions	
Unforgiving/bitterness	
Irresponsible	
Mental Confusion	
Mental Torment	
Fantasy escape (addictive thinking)	
Depression	
Enabler (over responsible)	
No moral compass	
Passive/aggressive behaviors	
Addictive behaviors (could be as simple as food compulsions)	
Self-mutilation (cutting)	
Self-destructive (alcohol/drugs/speeding/excessive gambling)	
Promiscuity	
High-risk behaviors	
Other:	
3) What good things did you have as a child? Let's make a positive shift and find the good	

things to dwell on and develop an attitude of gratitude.	
Childhood Comforts:	
Nice Friend	
Friendly personality	
Pets that I loved	
I wanted to do right	
Intelligent	
Good with my hands/crafty	
Hobbies	
Athletic	
Musically inclined	
Loving grandparent	
Stable adult influence	
Food	
Shelter	
Home	
Kind teacher	
Other:	

4) Who did you identify most with as a child? It is good to evaluate the people you admired. They have helped you build your identity. For example, have you practiced dysfunctional behaviors like one of your parents? This may have been an attempt to identify with them to win their approval. Shift your identity to a positive role model.	
Peers	
Absent Parent or abusive/enabling parent	
Older sibling	
Sports hero	
Historical hero	
Cult/gang leader	
Musician	
Do you identify with healthy or unhealthy individuals?	

Do you identify with those you were trying to please?	
Do you identify with one who was emotionally unavailable to you?	
Do you lead or follow a crowd?	

You could also evaluate your current relationships: marriage, children, employer, etc. Examine any dysfunction in your life. Focus on the good. Establish future goals for improvement within your control.

Now, reshape your future to look different from your past.

CHAPTER SIX

ENABLER'S BEHAVIORS

*Don't coddle irresponsibility and expect a
responsible outcome.*

Enabler's are typically people pleasers. They want what is good and right for their loved ones. Unfortunately, they manipulate people and circumstances to extract good behavior. This type of person is overly responsible and fosters irresponsibility in others. First, examine why you enable another person to stay in dysfunctional patterns. Then, look for yourself in the Enabler's Cycle. Next, discern how these same behaviors are exaggerated and used against you.

WHY DO YOU ENABLE A PERSON WITH ADDICTIVE BEHAVIORS?

Things to think about:
- Are you enabling another to stop your suffering?
- Are you protecting your reputation?
- Are you in denial? Do you think you are helping?

ENABLER'S CYCLE

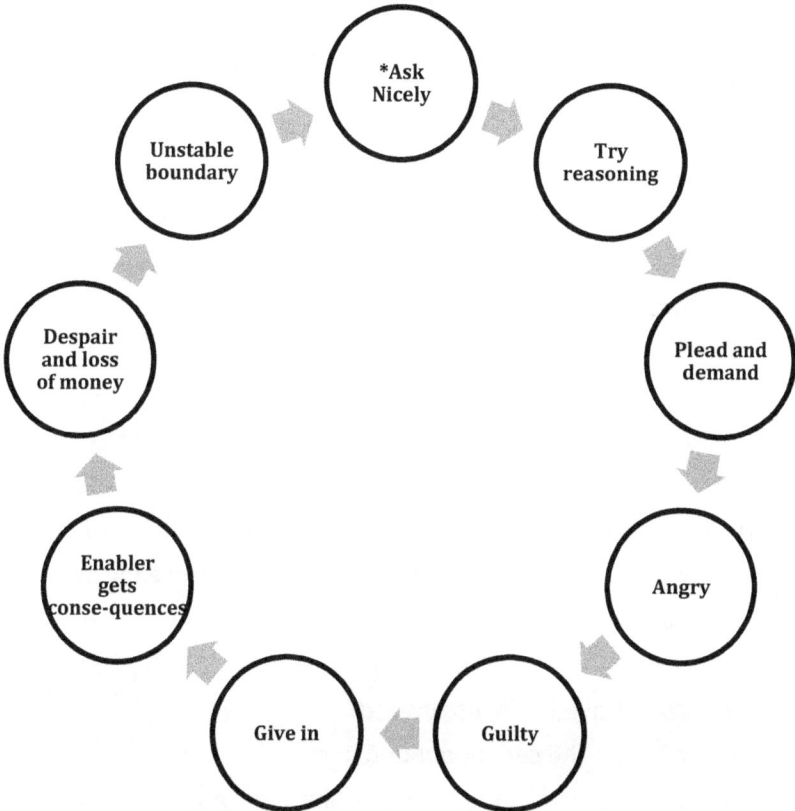

TRUTH FOR RECOVERY

1. Ask Nicely - This could be normal behavior in a healthy family. However, the enabler is expected to do all the work in a co-dependent family. While the person with SUD only responds or complies to avoid a hassle, avoid conflict or play you for their next fix.

    Truth:
    - Those with SUD usually do household chores or yard work, so you are indebted to them. Not because they love you and want to be a functional member of the family.
    - Often, they promise to do work and ask for pay upfront.
    - Next, they stick their hand out with an *entitlement attitude* and just ask for money.
    - They may be resentful, angry, grumbling and complaining to make you miserable for asking them to work.

2. Try Reasoning - This is where you must coax an adult to stop drinking, work for their income, and to plan for their expenses. The person with SUD will try this very reasoning on you. For example: If you don't bail me out of jail and get my car out of impound, I will lose my job and you will need to support me.

    Truth:
    - Who drove while intoxicated?
    - Who got the car impounded because of a DUI?
    - If you want them to learn the first time, it must hit them where it hurts with stern consequences.
    - If the first timer has to spend 6-12 months unraveling his consequences and paying his fine, he may not do it again.

3. Plead and Beg - This works both ways. If you pleaded and begged them to get out of bed this morning, they may plead and beg you for the car keys tonight.

Truth:

- Respect their boundaries. If they say no, accept their no.
- BUT...there are consequences to actions. One consequence for not getting up is getting their bed taken away. They can sleep on the floor, on the porch, in the car, at the shelter, under a bridge or they can get up and go to work tomorrow.
    - This takes a large amount of intestinal fortitude on our part to place boundaries and consequences and follow through to enforce boundaries and consequences.
    - You can't do this if you gave away all your power. You will have to diligently work a recovery plan to reclaim your own identity.

4. Angry - Passive/aggressive anger is destructive to relationships. Trust me this behavior is learned quickly and comes back to haunt you. Deal with your anger. The rule is patient, kind, but extremely firm with consequences for disobeying the house rules or rejecting your boundaries. Consistency is vital. If you are not in a place of power but are dominated by another individual, it is necessary to plan to do the hard work to empower yourself to change your situation. Also, your controlled anger is appropriate until you can extricate yourself from the toxic relationship. Use (silent and hidden) anger to motivate you to change and develop stronger boundaries.

Truth:

- Anger is to be used for protection and not to manipulate or coerce others emotionally.
- Anger can propel you to set up firm boundaries.
- Guard your tongue. Be kind, but firm.

Angry words don't bring healing.

5. Guilt - Work through your guilt and apologize and make restitution, if necessary.

   Truth:

   - Single parent, widowed parent, absent parent because of military, job duties, illness or divorce can cause a person to enable their loved ones to alleviate guilt.
   - Watch for the emotional guilt tactic. *An emotional guilt tactic is where the individual with SUD plays on your sympathy to embezzle or coerce money or property from you.*

6. Give in - Sometimes our boundaries are so pliable that the individual with SUD will just keep pushing buttons until they can find the right one to make you give in and submit to their demands.

Manipulation Hot Buttons

1. Whine, plead, cry, beg, pout
2. Angry, belligerent
3. Rationalizing
4. Blaming
5. Elevating selfish wants to a need
6. Accusing you
7. Bringing up your past
8. Turning your words against you
9. Bargaining with you
10. Emotionally withdrawing or isolating from you
11. Relationship suicide (Cutting you off if they can't get what they want)
12. Self-destructive behaviors: cutting, reckless driving, etc.
13. Denial of the root problem: focusing on superficial, temporal issues
14. Making you the problem

15. Gossiping and slandering

Truth:

- Detach emotionally from this person.
- Their brain is hijacked with drugs.
- They take **hostages** in relationships through emotional manipulation.

> *The quicker you can build walls around your heart...the sooner your decisions can be based upon what is best for your loved one long-term and not what is easiest for them right now.*

- Tough consequences may cause them to wake up and stop their behaviors. But first, YOU MUST **GET OUT OF THE WAY and stop RESCUING!**

7. Enabler Gets the Consequences - The more you relent and rescue the person with SUD, the less likely they are to learn. The more likely you will receive their consequences.

Truth:

- Staying on the pathway with a person with SUD will bring certain financial and emotional ruin and maybe even physically devastate your health.
- It may also take them longer to recover.
- The longer they are comfortable on a path of irresponsibility the more ingrained the dysfunctional behaviors become and the more devastating the consequences.
- If you have financial means, why not use them for a counselor or a reputable rehabilitation facility. *That isn't enabling, that is empowering your loved one to reclaim his life.*
- ****Each rescue is only a temporary fix.** The next consequence will be greater and greater, until eventually the consequences

will be so high, you will not be able to rescue them no matter how hard you try.

8. Despair and Loss of Money - When your finances are wasted, retirement savings gone and credit ruined, you will now be dependent upon others.

Truth:

- Disentangle yourself from this toxicity and salvage what you can before it is too late.
- Otherwise, you must find your own enabler to help rescue you from the consequences of impoverishment you received because of your enabling behaviors.
- You may even end up with a person who berates and belittles you day and night and have no viable means of leaving the situation.

The path of addiction with another always leads to loss and destruction

9. Unstable Boundaries - Enablers are moveable. They are tossed about like a little ship in a stormy sea. Their emotions are unstable. Their boundaries are unstable. Their decisions are unstable. Some enablers go without food or medicine. This is done so they can give their money away to an irresponsible person. Some enablers feel guilty if they don't give their money away.

Truth:

- You will soon lose your identity and become unable to control your addiction of enabling.
- Now find a stable, strong, dependable person to help guide you out of this mess!
- Trust this strong, dependable person to hold you accountable.

Poor boundaries are like quicksand.

Sad Truth: This person with substance use disorder is not your beloved son, daughter, father or brother. It is not them in front of you begging for money. It is alcohol. It is heroin. It is cocaine. Your loved one is long gone. Save your finances for a good, reputable counselor or rehabilitation program when they are ready to go. They will be ready sooner if they have no bed and are cold, wet and hungry.

<u>Rule:</u> **Never, never, never co-sign for them. Never place their expenses on your credit card. Never let them have your private financial information. Never get cash on your house to support them financially. Never bail them out of jail. Did I say…Never give them cash!!! If you feel you must pay child support, get a money order and address an envelope and mail it yourself. In case you didn't hear me…. Never ever give them cash! Most people with SUD cannot restrain themselves when they have cash in their hands. You may have signed their death warrant through overdose.**

> *Every time you give an a person with SUD cash you place another nail in their coffin. It is intense suffering to watch a loved one suffer.*

IRRESPONSIBLE ACTIONS ON THE PART OF AN ENABLER

- **Did you pay for an apartment, buy them a car and dress them up so they can pretend to be an honest citizen and find another unsuspecting victim to commandeer?**
- **This middle-class image will only lead to another beaten or abused lover, robbed employer, abortion, abandoned child, or**

even vehicular homicide.

- **If you let a person who has had a previous DUI drive your car, you are responsible for the outcome.**

There is a steep price to pay to give your loved one privileges he has not earned and has previously abused.

Now let's determine how entangled you are with another adult.

ENTANGLEMENT GAUGE

Evaluate yourself and how entangled you are with an irresponsible adult:

1. Providing Food

   (Taking them out to eat frequently or cooking for them without them having any responsibility to pay)

2. Providing Transportation

3. Gas card

4. Credit card

5. Car insurance

6. Health insurance

7. Paying car payment or buying a car for a person with a history of DUI's

8. Free (on demand) child care

9. Providing housing

10. Paying rent or buying them a home

11. Letting individual with substance use disorder live with you

12. Picking up after them

13. Doing their laundry

14. Paying utilities

15. Paying routine bills, cellphones, cable, internet, etc.

16. Buying nice clothes

17. Paying for haircuts

18. Making excuses for them

19. Co-signing for them	
20. Paying fees, fines, and other legal expenses	
21. Giving them false references for jobs	
22. Cashing checks for them or writing checks without reimbursement	
23. Paying unexpected bills: car repairs, doctor bills, prescriptions, etc.	
24. Paying for bad checks.	
25. Hiring attorneys to get them out of trouble. Paying bail.	
26. Berating and bullying other family members to enlist help for your loved one with SUD.	

This scale will help you identify how deeply you are entangled with an irresponsible adult. Enablers with a "stand them up" and "fix them up" philosophy make their loved one appear to be responsible. This sets them up nicely to prey on unsuspecting victims. These victims could be left beaten, pregnant and with their credit ruined within 4-6 months. It also sets the active substance users up to acquire jobs where they can abuse other employees and rob employers.

Next, let's identify the excuses enablers make for their loved ones in addiction. Over the next few days, listen to your speech. Are you making excuses for another person's irresponsible behaviors?

ENABLER'S MASTER EXCUSE MAKER LIST

1. You need to not be so hard on him.

2. You can't expect him to respect his teacher, boss, spouse, police officer, etc.
3. Everyone else has a car, he needs one too.
4. I'll pay half; you pay half.
5. You know what will happen if you don't pay that fine for him.
6. The poor thing can come and live with me.
7. He can get more student loans, so he can have his own place.
8. You should co-sign.
9. I paid for the car, now you pay the insurance.
10. He ran out of gas last night, you should get him a gas card.
11. He can't work, he is sick.
12. That job is too hard for him.
13. Being a painter is beneath him.
14. He can't do that job; he may hurt his knees.
15. Medicaid will take care of his needs.
16. He can't work, he is mentally ill.
17. He needs Social Security disability.
18. The military would be too demanding.
19. It's just a phase, he will grow out of it.
20. Now, don't upset him, just go along with it.
21. You hurt his feelings.
22. If he stays on pain medications four times a day, he will get more in his worker's compensation settlement and more for pain and suffering with his lawsuit.
23. You have to pay child-support, or he'll go to jail.
24. You are a horrible person; you just want him homeless.
25. He can't go to jail; he may get hurt.
26. He needs money in his pocket, so he can feel good about himself.
27. He said he was sorry. So, don't mention it again.

28. I am going to the rehabilitation center and get him because he doesn't need to be there.
29. I am going to bring him to your house.
30. He needs new shoes, now what are WE going to doing about it.
    What excuses do you hear yourself making for your loved one?

WHAT KIND OF AN EXAMPLE ARE YOU?

Half-truths vs. Honorable

As an enabler, I expect honorable behaviors from my loved ones. When they aren't honorable, I pretend. I pretend the half lie is the truth or compare my loved ones to others and say they doing better than them.

I rationalize:

- everyone bends the rules
- no one can be expected to be perfect
- it is good to look the other way to keep the peace, right?

The **truth** is that half-truths are lies. Lift up a standard for yourself and be honorable. Standing for honor takes a willingness to suffer for what is right. When conflict arises, only do the next honorable thing.

A standard will most likely bring conflict. Expect it.

HALF TRUTHS VS. HONORABLE

Half Truths	Honorable
Sometimes lie or speak half-truth to escape consequences for me or my loved one with SUD	Never lie Never cheat
Cheat on taxes or with insurance companies	Never steal
Do not correct an honest mistake if it is in my favor	Always honest Always kind and patient, but firm
Steal from credit card companies, & employers. Live above my means and have or need to file bankruptcy	Refuses to speak to liars and thieves until they repent
Motivated by Greed	Generous to responsible people and organizations
Motivated by selfishness (filing lawsuits for every fall or fender bender.)	Motivated by love (tough love, at times)
Motivated by what others think	Does what is right to protect a good reputation, but never compromises or goes along with what is wrong
Assist the one with SUD to file false worker's	Exhibits a strong work ethic Refuses to play manipulation

compensation claims.
 	
  Help manipulate doctors for their pain medication
 	
  Give them your medication
 	
  Drive them to the liquor store
	games
	
	  Refuses to allow anyone in the house who is under the influence of a mind-altering substance
	
	  Calls probation officers, police officers, and holds others accountable by arranging their arrest when they are stealing or out of control (This is love.)

Assisting loved ones to file lawsuits for circumstances they complicated with their substance use disorder	Developing the courage to stand alone and do what is honorable, truthful, and right
Base decisions on what I think I can do without getting caught	Does right, even when no one is looking
Have I been a bad example?	Working a plan to continue my recovery and to be held accountable to others for my decisions

> *If our morality is full of half-truths, we can expect an exaggeration of our poor example mirrored back in our face.*

Name one thing you could work on to be more honorable.

ENABLER'S DYSFUNCTIONAL THINKING

Enablers have dysfunctional thinking that needs corrected. There are behaviors and thought patterns we have learned that must be unlearned in recovery. Let's examine some dysfunctional thinking and its subsequent behaviors.

1. I must keep the peace at all cost.
2. I focus on pleasing others.
3. I neglect my own needs.
4. My anxiety and stress are unmanageable.
5. I rescue others from their consequences.
6. I have lost sight of the ability to say "no".
7. I am fearful of the consequences my loved ones might receive.
8. I frequently micro-manage and control little things.
9. I flip between being passive and aggressive.
10. No one respects my boundaries, so I stop trying.
11. I feel helpless and sometimes hopeless.
12. I want good for my loved ones.
13. I manipulate others and frequently bargain or bribe them.
14. I am driven by guilt.
15. I am ashamed of my loved one's dysfunction and hide it from others.
16. I protect irresponsible loved ones by making excuses for them.
17. I am a "fixer" and a "people-pleaser".
18. I am frequently perplexed about what direction to go and easily controlled.

19. My life is full of confusion.
20. I don't have the energy to reach out and get help for myself.

Identify Skewed Thinking

This skewed thinking needs corrected! Turn around five of these statements. Example: I don't have to keep the peace.

BELIEF SYSTEM QUESTIONNAIRE

Understanding our belief system that drives us to enable others is vital to recovery.

- **It is my fault they have substance use issues.** If I believe this, I need to explore why I feel guilty.

- **If I don't help them, they will have bad credit.** If I believe this, I need to understand bad credit is better than my indebtedness with nothing to show for it. Their bad credit is their responsibility.

- **Prison is too harsh.** If I believe this, I don't understand that confinement may be what they need to sober up, so they can make a responsible decision for their future. It will protect them from harming themselves and protect others from their abuse.

- **He isn't doing drugs anymore. He just has bad luck.** If I believe the cyclical emergency needs or hard luck stories are sincere, I don't understand the pattern of lies of the one caught in addiction will use to finance his substance use. He needs accountability and support to meet his recovery goals. He is not likely to do it alone.

- **Rehabilitation Centers aren't any good.** If I believe this, I don't understand how his addiction behaviors need to be interrupted and how he needs to be equipped with different thinking and coping skills. This can start in a rehabilitation center.

- **He can recover without support groups, sponsors and**

accountability. If I believe this, I don't understand the need for community and connectedness to find healing. Loved ones with substance use disorders need 3-5 years of continual recovery support. Many need a lifetime of support group accountability.

- **Recovery groups for me are a waste of my time.** If I believe this, I will not likely unravel the confusion in my life. I don't understand how my recovery will take minimum of 1-2 years of support to stop my anxiety, poor decisions, and identify my false beliefs. I also need help to change my over responsible behaviors and accountability to stop rescuing. Also, I need to learn to detach and develop healthy relationships. I am not likely able to do this alone.

- **I am grieving so hard or have so much anxiety when my loved one suffers that I must do something to relieve their problems.** This is not true. My anxiety will only return later. I need to receive support or counseling to understand where my responsibility begins and where it ends. I need to understand that their successful navigation of life's struggles will give them confidence to manage their life successfully without enablers.

- **I am their parent, spouse, or significant other, I need to make sure they are happy.** If I believe this, I don't understand that I am not responsible for another adult's morality, actions or happiness.

- **They will die in the gutter if I don't help them.** This may very likely be true. But they will be just as likely to die in your home with your enabling. Enabling only continues

their irresponsibility.
• **Once I decide to stop enabling, I can't help them at all.** This may or may not be true. It depends upon how much recovery work they are doing. Your decisions are your choice.

Stopping our enabling, models personal responsibility for our decisions.

Are there any other false beliefs you need to correct?

CHAPTER SEVEN:

ENABLER'S RECOVERY PLAN

*If there were no enablers, there would be less chaos
with those caught in addiction patterns.*

This is the recovery plan for an enabler.

1) I will not carry cash	
2) I will not give a person with SUD cash	
3) I will not be careless with personal information	
4) I will not trust my loved one with my debit/credit card	
5) I will not give my loved one my car keys	
6) I will not make any decisions alone regarding my loved one in addiction.	
7) I will let a trusted (non-sympathetic) accountability partner make decisions.	
8) I will be slow to speak and first think about what I am saying. .	
9) I will confess all lies to my accountability	

partner.	
10) I will confess any relapse to my trusted accountability partner and re-evaluate my boundaries with my loved one with SUD.	
11) I will make a responsible plan with my accountability partner or counselor and stick to it.	
12) I will not be easily accessible.	
13) I can turn my phone off at night.	
14) I will think of myself and my needs first and develop a self-care plan.	
15) I will not obsess about someone else's problems.	
16) I will refuse to be anxious about anything that hasn't happened.	
17) I will think of what is best for the long term.	
18) I will not make quick decisions.	
19) I will be courageous.	
20) I will turn the consequences of poor choices over to the person making those choices.	
21) I will reposition my energy to protecting innocent children or elderly.	
22) I will talk to one with SUD only with others present to hold me accountable.	
23) I will distance myself from anyone who isn't safe.	
24) I will recognize my anxiety, stop, take a deep breath and detach.	
25) I will not blame others for my loved one's	

problems.	
26) I will not make excuses for their poor choices.	
27) I will not guilt and shame others into accepting my loved one's poor behaviors.	
28) I will turn the responsibility for my loved one's problems back to them.	
29) I will allow others to correct my loved one with SUD.	
30) I will allow my loved one to suffer for poor choices.	
31) I will not intervene with court procedures.	
32) I will not pay fees and fines.	
33) I will observe actions and not words.	
34) I will seek out healthy relationships.	
35) I will develop healthy coping strategies.	

Add any other boundaries that may be needed to protect yourself from enabling one in active addiction. Identify any areas of weaknesses. If your loved one with SUD is not comfortable, clothed, fed, warm and dry, they will be less likely to want to continue in this destructive lifestyle.

GRACIOUS WORDS TO LOVINGLY UNRAVEL YOURSELF

1) I am so sorry for your troubles.
2) My plate is full right now, I don't think I can help you.
3) I am sorry. I have extra expenses this month and cannot help you.

4) You are so smart. I have complete confidence that you can figure this out.

5) So, what should you do differently to avoid this problem next time?

6) What are you learning from this experience?

7) How could you make better decisions?

Once you untangle from being responsible for other adult's problems, you can focus on taking personal responsibility for your well-being.

ACCOUNTABILITY QUESTIONS

Enablers, like our loved one's with SUD, are stuck in a pattern of behaviors. We often have blinders on and cannot fully see the path ahead. Each one of us need strong and courageous loved ones to help hold us accountable. Find a safe support group, trusted friend or counselor to help hold you accountable by asking you these questions regularly.

1. How would you rate your stress level?

2. Are you taking care of yourself: sleeping, exercise and healthy eating?

3. Are you taking care of your personal responsibilities: personal hygiene, cleaning, laundry, dishes, house, yard, and car?

4. Are you hiding anything?

5. Have you lied or made an excuse for your loved one this week?

6. Are you blaming someone else for your loved one's problems?

7. Are you arguing with someone who is trying to protect you?

8. Did you plan a decision and change your mind this week?

9. What was the decision? Were you coerced or bullied into changing your mind? Were you emotionally manipulated with crying or suicide threats?

10. Are you looking for co-enablers to be sympathetic and enable you so you may continue enabling your loved one with SUD?

11. Have you been alone or talked privately with your loved one to plot a rescue attempt for them?

12. How much have you discussed your loved one's problems with others?

Submission to an accountability partner is mandatory for recovery. An enabler is also caught in addictive and repetitive dysfunctional behavioral patterns, addicted to enabling their loved one with SUD or even their abuser. Recovery requires submission to an accountability partner, support group, and/or counselor.

> *Anyone caught in addictive behavioral patterns, must submit to authority and work a recovery plan because we cannot trust ourselves to make good decisions.*

We cannot trust ourselves to make the right decisions. *Most enablers have had their decision-making skills usurped through coercion, deception and manipulation.* It will take time to learn mature decision-making skills and to be able to trust yourself. This took me many years to accomplish.

I once heard a young person in recovery say, "It is harder to say 'no' to grandpa, than it is to drugs." Find a safe and trusted person to protect you. Submit to this authority and become transparent in all your actions. This will be a great recovery example for your loved ones to follow.

SELF-CARE

Self-care is vital for recovery. Enablers must see themselves as valuable. When we focus more on someone else's issues, we forget what we can control.

Self-Care
• Keeping yourself clean and presentable
• Keeping your environment clean
• Minding your own business
• Thinking healthy thoughts
• Speaking healthy words
• Eating properly
• Scheduling adequate sleep
• Scheduling exercise or enjoyable activities
• Setting firm boundaries with yourself and others
• Working on resolving bitterness, anger and past traumas.
• Exploring reasons for the need to rescue another.
• Dealing with any guilt or shame
• Seeking support groups and healthy friends.
• Rejecting all stupidity and irresponsibility.

DYSFUNCTIONAL COPING SKILLS

As an enabler, I utilized many dysfunctional coping skills. None of these produce lasting peace or emotional/relationship healing. They only perpetuate the cycle of confusion and chaos. Here is a list for you to identify where you may need to change your destructive behaviors.

Dysfunctional Coping Skills
• Yell, scream
• Pace or fret
• Ruminate on negative thoughts or events
• Mentally rationalize with an irrational person
• Mentally build a defense to prove your point
• Justify why your way is right and theirs is wrong
• Harboring bitterness and anger
• Living in denial; life is in confusion
• Impatient with others
• Negative self-talk
• Irritable and defensive
• Developing self-destructive behaviors
• Numbing emotional pain with mind-altering substances or prescription medications
• Isolation and withdraw
• Going places that I know are not healthy
• Anxiety that prevents enjoyment of the moment, keeps you in the past or future.
• Suicidal thinking
• Homicidal thinking

These are dysfunctional coping skills. Dysfunctional coping skills may change from day to day. The dysfunction may cause depression one day, anger the next and tears the next. These behaviors are destructive. Recognize them, then work a plan to do something different.

FUNCTIONAL COPING SKILLS

Be responsible for yourself and stop enabling. Then, you will have the energy to intentionally choose functional coping skills. Here is a list of functional coping skills that can nurture a peaceful life and prepare the way for healthy relationships.

Functional Coping Skills
• Exercise
• Hobbies
• Meditating on good thoughts
• Reading a book
• Taking a walk
• Visiting a sick friend
• Having pleasant conversation with a friend
• Purposefully enjoying the moment
• Developing a relationship with your higher power or safe inner self
• Going to a support group
• Going to a counselor
• Going to church or social gathering

- Joining a book club at the library
- Learning a new language or how to play an instrument
- Taking a class at the community college
- Going to the zoo or park
- Playing games with children
- Hiking, swimming, biking
- Going to work
- Doing the next honorable thing: making my bed, dishes, laundry, etc.

This is a list of potential confidence builders. It will get you outside of your inner pain and moving in another direction. Functional coping skills provide hope for you. Healthy coping skills can help you grieve, mourn, detach from things you cannot control and manage your own life. This is healthy.

CHAPTER EIGHT

MORE RECOVERY GUIDANCE

Rescuing is misguided mercy.

As a recovering enabler, it is important for life to be normal and peaceful. **Enablers dysfunctional attempt to achieve peacefulness is done by rescuing others from negative consequences from their poor choices. This only temporarily stops the chaos.**

To the person with SUD, mercy is seen as justification and acceptance of their poor behaviors and permission to continue their destructive path. In order to obtain the goal of peaceful, healthy relationships, person's with SUD and other enablers must be honorable and earn trust. Demanding others be responsible and earn trust will require a firm stance.

TRUST SCALE GUIDE

Never give an individual with SUD a temptation:

- Never leave your purse out.
- Hide your wallet.
- Hide your identity: Social Security card/Birth Certificate
- Count your checks and keep them under lock and key (they may take a couple checks in the middle or end of the checkbook.)
- Never give passwords.
- Never give security codes.
- Never give house key.
- Never allow them to make a purchase with your debit/credit card.
- Never leave prescription medications unlocked.
- Never give them a key to the car. (Hide keys when not in use.)
- Lock your bedroom door at night if they are in the house.
- Get an alarm system.

Individuals in recovery need to earn trust. This includes enablers as well as those with substance use disorder.

Are there any other boundaries needed in your situation?

Trust must be earned through true repentance. Unless you can identify the difference between true and false recovery, it is impossible to know if the person with SUD is beginning to recover or being enabled to stay on a destructive path again. As you recover from enabling and your loved one begins recovery, strong boundaries and distance in the relationship may be necessary.

TRUE RECOVERY   FALSE RECOVERY

Broken heart... grieving over their losses	Sorry for consequences, not behavior
Paying back anything stolen	Lots of emotions, crying, anger, mood swings
Setting boundaries to prevent themselves from falling back into old habits	Good behavior (temporarily) to make up for wrongs
Setting up accountability partners	Self-destructive thinking/behaviors
Being open and accountable in every area of life. Total transparency.	Saying "I am sorry." No plan to change.
Confessing past wrongs (with trusted person) Developing a plan for restitution.	Makes excuses (hiding full truth or blaming others)
Seeking help	Trying to weasel out of consequences

ENABLER'S JOURNEY RECOVERY PLAN

Sticking to a plan developed by counselor or authority	Refusing to talk over issues. "No one tells me what to do." Demands blind trust.
Walking daily in recovery.	Playing a good game, while they are learning to become a functional substance user.
Serving others without a desire for reward or a motive to manipulate others	Justifying self and grandiose thinking. They only do chores or favors with a motive to manipulate for selfish gain.
Placing structure in life. Make bed, take out trash, fold laundry, doing dishes, etc.	Avoids responsibility.
Schedule (work)	Embezzles money and cons elderly or weak for money. Misuses money allotted.
Earns trust one day at a time	Escalates emotions to cast confusion
Looks for a reason for past failures and working through past wounds to find healing	Creates crisis and diversion. (Self-destructive behaviors.) Runs away. Cuts self. Threatens suicide.
Finds healthy social settings	Returns to dysfunctional friends
Works towards developing boundaries to establish a safe environment	Resents submitting to authority
Corrects self by confessing	Double talks

and asks for forgiveness often.	
Speaks truth even if there are consequences	Lies
Accepts responsibility for actions	Blames
Provides for self and pays what has been borrowed Cares for children or elderly parents.	Selfish, bullies, dominates, plays a victim

Recovery without change is not recovery.

- True recovery is a turning away from destructive behaviors and then turning towards something valuable.
- Think of the last thing you said, "I am sorry" about and ask yourself, "Have I made provision in my life for a change?"

Sometimes we can't apologize:

- If I repent to a bully for upsetting them, I can expect they will test me with another *outrageous demand*.
- If this is the case, I must say no and set up firm boundaries.

Truth: Repentance should never give someone else the upper hand to manipulate you... again.

Remember: Love makes lasting changes...

Selfish people follow the direction of pleasing only themselves....

ENABLERS CAN REPENT FOR "ENABLING"

Here is what you could say:

"It has come to my attention that I have hindered you from becoming a functional and responsible adult by doing too much for you. I would like to say I am sorry for this. I intend to empower you to become as independent as possible." Now, develop a plan for one week, two weeks, one month, or six months to disentangle financially.

- Let them know that you will never be responsible financially for the consequences to their irresponsible behaviors.
- Let them know you will not hire an attorney or bail them out of jail. Leaving them in prison could save their life. Confinement can allow them to sober up so they can intelligently make a different choice for their life. This may be the best thing you can do for them. Seek counsel from others who know the situation well and are not easily manipulated.
- **Let them know any assistance plan you make with them is conditional. The plan will be abruptly abandoned if your loved one with SUD is not actively pursuing a recovery program.**

Develop a back bone and demand progressive recovery!

Caution:

- If they are resistant or argumentative, then say: "I have full confidence that you can do this." Give them phone numbers to rehabilitation facilities, sober living homes, shelters, food pantries and soup kitchens. Let them go. Some loved one's with SUD can't receive our help. They must find their own way.
- If you feel you are in danger and your boundaries will not be

respected, you may need to get legal counsel or contact the police to determine what options you may have to extricate them from your home or to get back what belongs to you.

- You may need to acquaint yourself with shelters for abused individuals.
- You may need to hide money until you have enough to gain your independence.
- You may need to borrow money to fully separate from an abusive situation.
- Seek legal counsel, if necessary.

METHODOLOGY TO FIND NEW ENABLERS

Warning: Any person with SUD who isn't interested in recovering will find other enablers. Prepare other friends and family members for the methodology of finding new enablers. It is also important to understand that you will receive resistance from individuals with SUD and other enablers. This resistance can escalate into toxic verbal or even physical abuse quickly. If this happens, let it increase your determination to pursue healthier relationships. Push back and maintain your right to a peaceful life.

These are classic methods people with SUD use to find new enablers.

1) Catchy pick-up lines at the grocery store, gas station, new employment, night club, strip club, drug/alcohol rehabilitation centers, etc.
2) Passionate and energetic with lots of dreams and goals.
3) Flatters and boast in their speech
4) Moves fast in relationships especially with sexual intimacy.

5) Quickly entangles new enabler financially
- Borrows money with promise to repay
- Many promises of future financial windfall: inheritance, workers' compensation claim, law suits, etc. *This is a lottery mentality.*
- Coaches new enablers on how to get student loans, credit cards, etc.
- Coaches new enabler on how to use emotional manipulation to embezzle money from their unsuspecting loved ones.

6) Pretends helplessness: Lavishes praise for meeting his desperate needs. He is temporarily down on his luck. You are his angel to rescue him from despair.
- Needs a place to do laundry
- Needs a couch to sleep on a few nights
- Needs a phone for potential employers to call
- Needs new shoes and clothes for potential job interview

7) Plays the victim like a champion.
- Replays old wounds
- Recants martyrdom and unselfish acts that weren't appreciated

8) Finds common ground with new enabler and charms their family
- **A chameleon**- He can gauge a situation and change his behavior: good companion, step-parent, cook, housekeeper, etc.
- Takes on the persona of whoever he is around and becomes who they want him to be.
- Deludes significant others that could protect the new

enabler.
- Slurs family and friends that are warning you or are suspicious of him.
- Separates you from anyone who isn't fooled by him and who could protect you.

Any good behavior is temporary.

The good behaviors disappear when you:
- Question them.
- Don't play the game.
- Set a boundary

AVOIDING PITFALLS

Test all new relationships.
- Go slow
- Set up accountability and expectations
- Turn them over to stronger people that can hold them accountable if they have a history of substance use disorder or domestic violence (support groups, sponsors, counselors, etc.)
- Expect 3-5 years of solid recovery and employment before considering a serious relationship with them.
- Question past behaviors
- Ask them to acknowledge their shortcomings
- Don't rescue them from consequences of previous poor choices or give them sympathy
- Ask other people about their history

- Expect other adults to be responsible for their own financial needs
- Talk to ex-mates or ex-lovers
- Don't overlook lies.
- Set firm boundaries

ADVICE FOR THE EMPATHETIC

If a person will not accept a boundary, or a "no" response, run quickly. If they quickly become emotionally unstable in stressful situations, step back from the relationship and observe their behaviors for 6 months. If they are your true love, they will still be there. If they are only looking for an enabler, they will move on and you will be spared the nightmare.

Empathy Queen

Are you an **empathy queen**? Do you feel everyone's pain and need to fix other people's problems? ***This beautiful heart of compassion is a good thing, until it is not.*** When compassion serves others in need and brings you fulfillment and purpose it is good. But when compassion becomes distorted and makes us vulnerable to abuse, it becomes a thief.

Did you get that?

Compassion out of balance becomes a thief.

It robs you of the joy of giving and makes others dependent. It robs others of the potential to become healthy and confident individuals. The give and take of a fluid relationship can quickly advance into a tug of war of demanding rescue from the consequences of destructive decisions. This emotionally stunts an adult into a perpetual adolescent role. Adolescence is the time where youth are still dependent and pushing back to find healthy independence and internal controls to govern their own behaviors. These internal controls are developed as they receive consequences for poor choices. These are valuable life lessons to prepare them for adulthood. But, when an adult is stuck in this immature stage of shirking responsibilities, they regress in development and become perpetually immature.

If our compassion breaks the fall of the consequences of another adult's poor choices, we usurp life experience meant to shape them into functional individuals of society. Instead, they become entitled just like the leech who takes and takes some more.

CONCLUSION

The enabler's recovery work can be accompanied with unbearable grieving and loss. Do not indulge yourself in sorrow or self-pity (except in small portions) or you will go insane. If your loved one refuses recovery, it may seem worse than death. There will be no closure. There will be no end to the grieving until you totally detach and distance yourself. Which is certainly not optimal, but after a decade or two may be your only viable option for emotional survival, enjoyment of life and normalcy for you, your other loved ones and the children involved.

The sooner an enabler stops enabling, the sooner your loved one may choose to seek recovery. Remember to find the good and detach from the decisions that aren't within your control. Only you know the right decision for you and your family. Hopefully, this book has given coaching insights and set up parameters for a healthier and safer relationship with an emotionally immature individual with substance use disorder. Take your time making decisions and reach out for support and counsel. Only you can be responsible for your decisions and know which ones are healthy for you.

Fight for your freedom and let no one steal it from you again. Let others own their own problems. After you are free, be careful to continue working your recovery plan. Otherwise, you will begin to find others who are lost or broken and enable them and be entangled all over again.

May you be free to love and free to find love. May you find your recovery. Recovery is doing the right thing and not the easy thing.

Loved one's with SUD need more than an enabler can give them.

Finally, if someone can rob you of your peace and steal your joy, they have way too much power over you. Work through the upcoming Enabler's Journey Detachment Plan: Enabler's Journey Recovery Series Book 2. The Detachment book contains 12 Healthy Detachment Principles to care for yourself and Understanding your Helpless Trap; and Setting Relationship Goals. The book, also, coaches you in assisting your recovering loved one by developing a Financial Empowerment Plan; Immediate, Intermediate and Long-Term Recovery Goals; and other Healthy plans for Caring for your actively recovering loved one with SUD. Learn to detach from suffering and reclaim your power.

REFERENCES

Alcoholics Anonymous. (1938). Akron, OH: Alcoholics Anonymous.

Dictionary by Merriam-Webster: America's most trusted online dictionary. (n.d.). Retrieved from https://www.merriam-webster.com/

How Al-Alon works for families and friends of alcoholics. (2008). Virginia Beach, VA: Al-Anon Family Group Headquarters.

Kubler-Ross E. (1985). *On death and dying.* Enfield, N.S. W.: Royal Blind Society.

AUTHOR'S BIOGRAPHIES

Angie G. Meadows graduated from St Mary's School of Nursing as a Registered Nurse, Marshall University with a Bachelor's in Nursing and Ohio State University with a Master's in Nursing. She has worked at multiple hospitals in multiple capacities. Angie has been a keen observer of human behaviors as she has dealt with enablers and loved one's with in SUD over the years. She is currently a wife, mother, speaker and writer. Her favorite past time is quilting.

Dr Perry Meadows graduated from Marshall University with a Bachelor of Science in chemistry, Master of Science in Biological Sciences, and Doctorate of Medicine. Dr. Meadows completed his internship and residency at Marshall University School of Medicine in Family Practice and is a Fellow of the American Academy of Family Physicians. Dr. Meadows also received his Juris Doctor from Salmon P. Chase College of Law, Northern Kentucky University and M.B.A. from Regis University. Dr. Meadows speaks on a local, regional, and national level on topics related to substance use disorder. He is active in working with various community organizations across Central Pennsylvania in issues related to behavioral health and substance use disorder.

Sarah J Meadows graduated from Liberty University with a bachelor's degree in psychology. She has worked in the public-school system as a Therapeutic Day Treatment Counselor. She is currently pursuing a Master degree in Clinical Mental Health Counseling. Sarah enjoys her friends and her beloved corgi.

OTHER RESOURCES BY THE AUTHORS

A Thousand Tears: An Enabler's Journey

ISBN 9781732810204

Identifying the Enabler's Cycle and our conflict with individuals with addiction. Identifying a manipulator, devourer, or toxic relationship in our life and learning to confront and detach. This book is a useful tool in dealing with person's with SUD or abusive loved ones. It also includes multiple self-assessment tools: Enabler's paradigm, entanglement gauge, anxiety quotient, trust scales, and much more.

An Enabler's Journey: A Christian Perspective

ISBN 9781732810211

This is almost identical to *A Thousand Tears: An Enabler's Journey* except the book contains more than a 100 Scripture references to validate the ancient principles of dealing with problems.

Enabler's Journey Detachment: Enabler's Journey Recovery Series Book 2

ISBN 9781732810228

Angie G Meadow MSN; Perry Meadows MD, & Sarah J Meadows BS

This is book one of a recovery workbook series. It guides individuals and clients to understand enabling behaviors and evaluate their current participation in perpetuating the addiction cycle of others. The enabler will learn to recognize the cycle of enabling, entanglement, excuses and beliefs that handicap an enabler from recovery. It also coaches in the courage needed for detaching from destructive people and circumstances we cannot control. The book includes an enabler's recovery plan, accountability questionnaire, self-care program and a plan for identifying unhealthy and healthy coping strategies. It will also guide the recovering enabler to determine a level of safe involvement with a loved one caught in addiction patterns and how to identify true and false recovery, rebuild trust, and avoid the snare of another enabling relationship.

The book has 5 chapters from the original A Thousand Tears: An Enabler's Journey Book and 3 new chapters for personalized recovery. It is a short 100 pages with room for journaling and reflective thinking. It is specific for the person whose life is in chaos and they cannot focus on in-depth material. This book lends itself to small group sharing or can help counsellors guide enablers to build an individual recovery plan.

Journaling and Notes

Angie G Meadow MSN; Perry Meadows MD, & Sarah J Meadows BS

ENABLER'S JOURNEY RECOVERY PLAN

Angie G Meadow MSN; Perry Meadows MD, & Sarah J Meadows BS

ENABLER'S JOURNEY RECOVERY PLAN

Angie G Meadow MSN; Perry Meadows MD, & Sarah J Meadows BS

ENABLER'S JOURNEY RECOVERY PLAN

Angie G Meadow MSN; Perry Meadows MD, & Sarah J Meadows BS

ENABLER'S JOURNEY RECOVERY PLAN

Angie G Meadow MSN; Perry Meadows MD, & Sarah J Meadows BS

ENABLER'S JOURNEY RECOVERY PLAN

Angie G Meadow MSN; Perry Meadows MD, & Sarah J Meadows BS

.

ENABLER'S JOURNEY RECOVERY PLAN

Angie G Meadow MSN; Perry Meadows MD, & Sarah J Meadows BS

ENABLER'S JOURNEY RECOVERY PLAN

Angie G Meadow MSN; Perry Meadows MD, & Sarah J Meadows BS

ENABLER'S JOURNEY RECOVERY PLAN

Angie G Meadow MSN; Perry Meadows MD, & Sarah J Meadows BS

ENABLER'S JOURNEY RECOVERY PLAN

Angie G Meadow MSN; Perry Meadows MD, & Sarah J Meadows BS

ENABLER'S JOURNEY RECOVERY PLAN

Angie G Meadow MSN; Perry Meadows MD, & Sarah J Meadows BS

Angie G Meadow MSN; Perry Meadows MD, & Sarah J Meadows BS

www.ingramcontent.com/pod-product-compliance
Lightning Source LLC
Chambersburg PA
CBHW032007040426
42448CB00006B/523